FACING
LIONS

RISK TAKERS

FACING LIONS

God's Amazing Works
in the Days of the Early Church

J.R. WILLIAMSON
R.M. FREEDMAN

CF4•K

10 9 8 7 6 5 4 3 2 1
© Copyright 2013 J.R. Williamson and R.M. Freedman
ISBN: 978-1-78191-153-2

Published by Christian Focus Publications,
Geanies House, Fearn, Tain, Ross-shire,
IV20 1TW, Scotland, U.K.
www.christianfocus.com
E-mail: info@christianfocus.com
Cover design by Daniel van Straaten
Cover illustration by Neil Reed

Character and chapter illustrations by Neil Reed
Maps by Neil Reed except for map on page 41
by Fred Apps
Printed and bound by Bell and Bain, Glasgow

CONTENTS

LET'S GET STARTED

Have you ever gone to see the lions in a zoo? Usually it's a pretty boring exhibit. Otters may swim around and chase each other, mountain goats may leap around over the rocks, but lions pretty much look like big house cats. They lie around in the sun, and occasionally get up and stroll about, or do a bit of personal grooming. They have the air of someone who is just killing time until lunch is served. They are not really very frightening, are they?

But that's because they're in a zoo. They're on one side of a big barrier, and you're on the other, maybe taking photos and thinking that the otters were more entertaining.

What if they were free? What if you somehow got left behind at the zoo at night, and a big 400-pound lion got loose and was prowling around all the paths, looking for an easy after-dinner snack? He roars, and every creature in the zoo, and for miles around, freezes for an instant in dread. Is he after me? How far away is he? How fast can I run?

The Bible says that the devil, who is the adversary of all Christians, prowls around like a roaring lion, looking for someone to devour. He wants to bring down God's people however he can. Sometimes he uses their own sins to make them stumble and fall, and other times he uses false teachers to fight against the truth, or a wicked government. Back in the days of the early church, when the devil stirred up the Roman officials to persecute God's people, actual lions were sometimes used against believers! The Christians who refused to betray Christ were sent into arenas to be torn to pieces by wild animals.

The devil wants Christians to become fearful and ineffective, and he especially wants them to forget to trust God. He knows that a Christian who remembers that God created everything out of nothing, and that he is loving and merciful will be bold. That Christian will not be terrified by anything as trifling as lions or wicked men.

This is why God tells his people that if they "resist" the devil by being "steadfast in the faith" (1 Peter 5:9) the devil himself will flee from them, as if they had suddenly turned into fierce predators—or great warriors. God does not ask his people to face their enemies without first giving them all the armor and weapons they need to be strong: they are given belts of truth, shields of faith, helmets of salvation, and their offensive weapon is the very Word of God "living and powerful, and sharper than any two-edged sword" (Hebrews 4:12).

So come, meet some men and women of the early church who loved and obeyed God and bravely stood against the devil and his followers. Meet the Christian believers who defied emperors in defense of God's truth, looking always to the Lord Jesus, who is himself the Lion of the Tribe of Judah, the Lord of Lords and the King of Kings.

SPEAKING BOLDLY AT THE BATH HOUSE:
The Apostle John (d. AD 101)

There have been many great and godly men named John down through church history, but the one I want to tell you about here is the Apostle John. In the gospel that he wrote, he often called himself "the disciple who Jesus loved," but he had other names—for one thing, Jesus himself called John and his brother James "Boanerges," which means "sons of thunder," because of their hot tempers. And In church history, he is often called John the Evangelist.

John lived longer than most of the other apostles, many of whom were killed when they were still fairly young. But though John was not martyred for his faith, in some ways he had an even greater trial to endure. The Bible tells us that God's enemy, the devil, "prowls around like a lion" seeking to destroy true believers. He likes to appear "as an angel of light" to deceive people—and he has many, many followers, who have turned away from God's truth and instead join with the devil in trying to hurt God's people. Even in the very early years, false teachers were sneaking into the church, inventing pretty-sounding lies to lead people away from the truth. The New Testament was not yet all written down, so it was harder for Christians to know just what was true about some very important doctrines, which were new and wonderful, but also sometimes difficult to understand.

These false teachers claimed to be "Christian," but denied things that the Bible taught, and had very clever arguments for what they were teaching. Like many men and women today, they weren't content just to say "I don't believe Christianity is true" and walk away. They did not want to turn their backs on Christianity entirely, even though they didn't like what Jesus Christ said about themselves or their sins. Unfortunately, instead of admitting that they were wrong, they took a few things that they liked from

Scripture and then mixed in a bunch of their own bad ideas. This still happens today. In the early days of Christianity these bad ideas were often called "new revelations" or "secret truths" by the wicked men who invented them. There were lots of different people who taught that you could find secret knowledge through them, and they were called "Gnostics" (Nah-sticks), which is from a Greek word for knowledge. The church eventually saw that the teachings of the Gnostics were heresies. Heresies are teachings that are so harmful that to receive and believe them will lead to eternal damnation (2 Peter 2:1). So, being a teacher of heresies (a heretic) was a deadly serious thing. It meant you were teaching people things that would lead them to hell, and that you yourself were under God's angry judgment.

When John was still alive, he had to fight against some of these false teachers, or heretics. John loved the Lord Jesus above anybody, and he hated it when someone came along and told lies about who he was. One of the men that did this was named Cerinthus (Sir-enth-us). Cerinthus taught that Jesus wasn't really the Christ, the Son of God, but just a human man, and that something called the "christ spirit" had lived in Him for a little while, but then left Him at the end, so that He died as just a normal man. The Gospel of John and the short letters of John teach the truth about Jesus, against the lies of Gnostics like

Cerinthus. However, this false teacher continued to ignore the truth and teach his lies. When you read the Gospel of John, you can't help but notice how often he mentions God's love for mankind, and John has even been called the Apostle of love, because he cared so much for believers and unbelievers alike. But John was also that "son of thunder" in some ways, and he knew that God's wrath against those who reject his Son is very real.

John had a young friend and disciple named Polycarp, who told of one time when John's love for God's truth and hatred of false teaching made him

refuse to take a bath! In the days when the Apostles lived in the Roman Empire, people didn't take baths as often as we do today, but when they did, they went to a place in town where the men bathed in one area and the women in another. It was sort of like an indoor swimming pool or hot tub, but a public one where you never knew who you might run into. One day, John went to the bath with some of his friends. But as they started to prepare to get in, they saw Cerinthus! John had warned believers about not letting dangerous false teachers into their house or church to try to peddle their lies: "If anyone comes to

you and does not bring this doctrine, do not receive him into your house nor greet him; for he who greets him shares in his evil deeds" (2 John 10-11 NKJV). Well, John wasn't in his own house that day, so he couldn't shut the door in Cerinthus' face—but he certainly didn't greet him! He didn't just pretend not to see him, either. In fact, John took Cerinthus' lies so seriously, that when he saw him there, he turned and bolted for the nearest exit, urging his friends to come along, "before the bath-house falls down, because Cerinthus, the enemy of the truth, is in here!"

Now, as far as we know God was merciful to his enemy that day and didn't bring the bath house down on his head, but from this story we get a glimpse of how strongly John the Evangelist felt about those who told lies about his Savior.

Even after John had grown old and died, he continued to "fight on" through his writings, and also through the men he had trained to be future leaders in the church there in Asia Minor.

AWAY WITH THE ATHEISTS!:
Polycarp (d. AD 156)

Polycarp was a disciple of John and "sat at his feet" to learn from him, just as John had "sat at the feet" of the Lord Jesus. When he was older, he became a pastor in Smyrna, which is modern-day Turkey. We don't know very much about Polycarp, except that he lived a long life of faithful service to Christ and was dearly loved by his church. We also know he had the same bold spirit as his mentor, John. During this time, there were false teachers who claimed that Jesus was not truly man as well as truly God. One of these was named Marcion. When Marcion met Polycarp, perhaps knowing that Polycarp had been warning Christians about the things Marcion had been teaching, he said, "Do you know who I am?" Polycarp didn't beat around the bush, but replied promptly, "I do know you ... you are the first born of Satan!"

So, the infant church was attacked and tested from its very earliest days. Almost all the major figures of the New Testament died at the hands of the government as martyrs, and over the next three centuries hundreds of thousands more followed them in death for believing on Jesus without compromise.

The Romans worshiped many so-called "gods," like Zeus and Hermes which we read about in the Bible (Acts 14:11-13). They also often worshiped the emperor (who they called "Caesar") as if he was a god. They would take a little pinch of sweet smelling incense as a sacrificial worship offering and they were required to declare that "Caesar is Lord!"

Believers in Jesus knew that all of these "gods" were made up and didn't exist, and that the emperor was certainly just a man and not "Lord" and master of men's souls. They refused to worship him or these other gods, even though everyone else either truly believed in these gods or were willing to play along to keep out of trouble. It's amazing to think that because they declared that there is only one true God, the Christians were called "atheists"! Many of the Roman leaders wanted to force all the so-called "atheists" to accept the false gods of Rome as true gods—or at least to say that they did! Since Polycarp was a beloved leader of the church in Smyrna, he was a special target of the government. They ordered his arrest and demanded that he claim that these gods were real.

This particular persecution was the fourth of the ten most well known periods, and it was under a man that the world, amazingly, still admires today. His name was Marcus Aurelius, and people called him a "philosopher king." Though he did good in some areas of his rule, he hated and tried to wipe out the Christians, ordering the slaughter of thousands throughout the empire.

Polycarp was one of the many Christian leaders hunted down by the emperor's soldiers. At first, when he learned that the authorities were coming to arrest him, Polycarp wished to stay in town, but his friends begged him to flee. He did hide in various places for a time, but soon he came to a certain cottage and refused to run again, saying, "The Lord's will be done." The soldiers frightened a slave boy into telling them where Polycarp was hiding. When they arrived, they found Polycarp peacefully asleep upstairs in his bed, trusting God to take care of him.

When the soldiers saw Polycarp, they were very surprised to find that the fugitive they had such a hard time finding, was no quick and stealthy criminal, but just a frail old man—and a very kind old man at that! Instead of being frightened and begging them to let him go, or being angry and cursing them, he had a large meal prepared for them, and only asked that he be allowed to pray for an hour before he left with them. To their amazement, he prayed not only for himself and other believers, but for the very men who had come to arrest him, so that some of the

soldiers began to feel terrible about what they had been sent to do.

All the way to the arena, his captors tried to persuade Polycarp to turn his back on the Lord Jesus. "What can be the harm in saying that Caesar is Lord?" they asked him. All he needed to do was burn a little incense to the emperor, and he could save his own life, and spare his friends much grief. Some of the men who tried to talk Polycarp into betraying his Lord did so out of a true desire to see him saved

from a cruel death in the arena, but others knew that if they could get such an important Christian leader to deny the Lord Jesus, many others in the church would lose heart and deny him as well. When their arguments failed to move Polycarp, they began to threaten him, but Polycarp was not impressed by either the "friendly" words or the threats, and only replied, "I am not going to do what you tell me to do." By the time he had reached the arena, the men saw that this gentle and kind old man was also stubborn about who he would worship!

The arenas were large theaters used for sports and plays. They were also used to display the punishments of those who refused to do what the emperor wanted them to do. Many Christians were sent to die in these arenas, as a "show" for the Roman people. Picture a big sports stadium, only instead of you and your family and friends going to watch a football or a baseball game, you are going to see a bunch of people suffer and die, being attacked by wild animals or armed warriors or both! Maybe they are murderers and robbers, or maybe they are just the sort of people you can't stand for some reason, like those annoying Christians, who were always telling you that your favorite gods didn't really exist. The suffering of others had become the main entertainment of the Roman Empire.

So Polycarp was brought to an arena, and since he was such a well-known Christian leader, great crowds of people had come to see what would happen to him. The place was incredibly noisy, and when they finally saw Polycarp himself brought in, the uproar only got worse. Here would be a great show!

When the proconsul (who was like a governor for that region) saw Polycarp standing before him, he asked the prisoner to confirm that he truly was Polycarp. It seems that, like the soldiers before him, he probably had trouble believing that this elderly man was the bold preacher that had been so difficult to silence. Then, the proconsul also began trying to convince him to save himself. "Have respect to your age," he advised him. Why should Polycarp suffer as a feeble old man? He told Polycarp all he needed to do was show his loyalty to the emperor, and condemn all the other Christians in the arena by saying, "Away with the atheists!"

Polycarp had stood quietly listening to this point. But when the proconsul commanded him to condemn the Christians as atheists, he decided to speak. He turned his eyes, not toward his fellow followers of Jesus, but to the crowd all around him, then looked up to heaven and said "Away with the atheists!"

This was not what the Romans wanted to hear! The proconsul must have been angered by this, since it made him look foolish. Polycarp had turned the ruler's words against him - those who didn't believe in the only true God and his Son Jesus Christ were the real atheists! But he still tried to get Polycarp to betray Christ. He knew that if he could get this one old man to turn against his Lord out of fear for his life, it would be a huge blow to the church, and wouldn't the emperor be pleased with that!? "Swear to Caesar, and curse Christ, and I will let you go," promised the proconsul.

At this, Polycarp looked straight at the Roman official who, like Pontius Pilate years ago, thought he held the life or death of a certain Prisoner in his hands, not knowing that without God's permission he had no power at all (John 19:10-11). But Polycarp knew who really ruled the world, and he loved the Lord Jesus, as his teacher John had done before him. "I have served him eighty-six years," Polycarp told the proconsul, "and he has never wronged me. How, then, can I blaspheme my King, who saved me?"

Even then, the proconsul did not give up. He threatened Polycarp with being thrown to wild beasts, and when that did not frighten him, with being burned to death. To this Polycarp replied that the Romans could only threaten with a fire that burned for a little while and then went out, because they were not aware of the fires of coming judgment and everlasting punishment that await the ungodly. Then he bravely challenged them, "But why do you delay? Come, do what you will."

Realizing he could not change Polycarp's mind, the proconsul had it proclaimed to the crowd that the prisoner had "confessed his guilt" by declaring himself a Christian. The crowd shouted with anger: they wanted Polycarp eaten by lions, they wanted him burned alive! They rushed to help get the wood for the fire, eager to see the end of this stubborn "atheist" who spoke against their gods. When the Romans tried to nail Polycarp to the pole surrounded by all the wood, Polycarp told them that the Lord who would give him strength to endure the fire would also give him help to remain there without nails or ropes to hold him. As he stood there, he prayed, praising God for Jesus and for his salvation, and thanking the Lord that he would be considered worthy to be a martyr for his Savior. Then they lit the fire, and he died while all around him the pagans cheered. This was the way in which Polycarp entered into glory and won a reward which none could take away from him.

So it was that Polycarp's martyrdom did not weaken the church, but strengthened its commitment. His church wrote a letter describing his courage, as an encouragement to Christians in other parts of the world. Believers grew even bolder in following Jesus Christ who "when he was reviled, he did not revile in return; when he suffered, he did not threaten, but continued entrusting himself to him who judges justly" (1 Peter 2:23 ESV). Not only that, but many in that bloodthirsty crowd were unwillingly impressed by Polycarp's behavior throughout his trial. They marveled at the difference between Christians and unbelievers in the way they faced death. Who can doubt that some of them must have begun to seek the reason for the difference, and at length become believers themselves?

Polycarp's martyrdom had yet another effect, by the grace of God: almost at once, the fierce persecution of Christians in that area came to an end, as if even hardened "athiests" had been touched by his gracious spirit, and made ashamed of their hatred for a kind old man. Polycarp in his life had sought the good of mankind, and had even gone to his death praying, not for their destruction, but their salvation.

DEVOTIONAL THOUGHT

Persecution has afflicted the Christian church from its very beginning. Those who trust and follow the one true God have always had to face opposition. Even if you go back into Old Testament times you will discover the names of believers who were willing to suffer and die rather than betray the one true God.

Shadrach, Meshach and Abednego were three friends who refused to worship the statue of the Babylonian King. They were thrown into a fiery furnace as punishment. Miraculously they survived. Not even a hair on their heads was burnt. The aroma of smoke wasn't even on their clothes.

In the New Testament, the Apostle Paul was often in fear of his life from beatings and whippings. He was finally arrested and imprisoned and later was martyred for his faith.

Jesus Christ has said that we're not to be surprised when this happens. The world hates him, so it will hate his followers too. We must trust in God. He is in control. His justice will never end. Jesus will return one day and God's people will rise from the dead to live an everlasting life free from suffering and persecution.

FACT FILE

Smyrna was an ancient city located at a strategic point on the Aegean coast of Anatolia. It was an easy area to defend and had good inland connections. The ancient city is located at two sites within modern Turkey. There are several explanations for how this city got its name but it is interesting to note that Smyrna is also an ancient Greek word for myrrh. Myrrh is a gum/resin that is harvested from trees in the Middle East. It has been used throughout history as a perfume, incense and medicine.

THE WEAK MADE STRONG:

Blandina (d. AD 161)

During the same period of persecution under Marcus Aurelius, thousands of Christians were martyred in Gaul, which is what we call the country of France today. There were two church communities in particular that suffered persecution, the brethren in Vienne and in Lyon. Whoever knew and loved Jesus was in trouble with the government, whether they were rich or poor, adults or children.

Of all the Christians who suffered, the most shining example of steadfast faith was Blandina. Blandina was a slave, but the lady for whom she worked was a Christian and a member of the church along with Blandina. It often happened that servants and slaves told their masters about the Lord, or masters their servants, and so the gospel spread between different classes of people. In Blandina's case, we don't know who was first converted, but certainly she and her mistress encouraged each other in the faith as the church began to come under fire.

When Christians began to be arrested and taken to be killed, the church worried about the poor servant girl, Blandina. The emperor, Marcus Aurelius, had sent instructions that Roman citizens who would not renounce Christ, should be beheaded, but that all those who were poor and unimportant should be tortured until they confessed to all sorts of crimes in order to escape further punishment. Blandina was so small and weak that the church thought it would be especially hard for someone like her to endure and hold fast to her faith in the Lord Jesus.

But God showed how he is able to take the weakest person and make them strong and mighty for him. The day came when Blandina and her mistress, as well as many other Christians, were arrested and led away to be tried. The soldiers took her and led her to a large stadium or arena, similar to the one that Polycarp had been taken to. Then, they began to beat and do many painful things to Blandina. They told her she should curse Jesus Christ. They accused her and the Christians of doing many very wicked and vile things. But she would only say in response, "I am a Christian, and there is no evil done among us."

For a whole day, from morning to evening, these wicked Roman officials had her tortured, trying to make her deny her Lord, and tell lies about how Christians behaved. But though the emperor and his men might despise a lowly slave, God chose her as his special witness to show how he helps his people who trust in him. When the men started to whip and flog Blandina, they expected she would quickly give up and agree to whatever they said about her and her Christian friends. Instead, the day dragged on and it was the soldiers who gave up. The men actually wore themselves out and quit for the day! They were astonished at what she had endured, knowing that just one of the many tortures they had put her through would normally have killed a man, let along a small, frail girl.

Blandina and others were sent back to the prison to wait until another day of "games," as the Romans called these cruel acts performed before pagan crowds who delighted in the death of Christians.

One of the ways that persecutors tried to mock and dishearten Christians was through putting them on a cross, making fun of them and of their Savior. The next day that Blandina was in the arena, they did this to her, and released wild beasts into the stadium to devour her. Several other Christians were there as well.

But, to everyone's amazement, the beasts did not attack her. And instead of intimidating the Christians through mockery, her fellow disciples looked and saw her on the cross, and were strengthened. It made them remember Christ, and how he had suffered for them, as they were suffering. It inspired them greatly, and just as greatly it bewildered the enemies of the gospel.

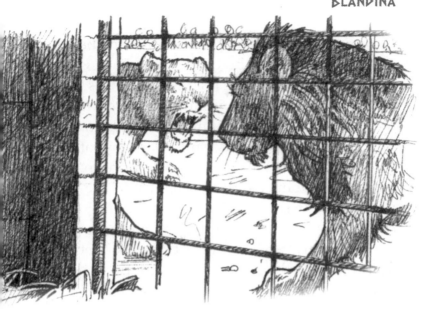

The other Christians knew that suffering was one of the ways they could follow in the footsteps of Christ, their Master, and Blandina's quiet endurance was an example to them to be like lambs led to the slaughter. They also knew that these things they were suffering would end as soon as their life ended, and they would receive an eternal crown of glory for faithfulness to their beloved Savior. Several died that day, seeing their sister Blandina holding fast, and no doubt thinking in their hearts that if God could give a little slave girl the strength to endure, he would surely help them as well. Blandina lived on, for the Lord had determined to show his power in her and she was put back in prison until the next games were held.

During these weeks of persecution Blandina's strong spirit ministered to the other imprisoned Christians from the first day to the last. Everyone was surprised and amazed as she held on in the prison, day after day, with broken bones and countless wounds and bruises. The soldiers were baffled. On the last day, after some of the older Christians were killed, a fifteen-year-old boy named Ponticus was brought into the arena as well. As he was being tortured and dying, Blandina comforted and encouraged him, and was for him like a mother. She helped her Christian brothers and sisters to fight the good fight of faith by urging them to hold fast to their confession until the end.

Having held on physically and spiritually through all these torments, Blandina died at last as well. The brethren who escaped persecution to tell of these events wrote a letter to other churches which describes Blandina's last moments. They said:

"And, after the scourging, after the wild beasts, after the roasting seat, she was finally enclosed in a net, and thrown before a bull. And having been tossed about by the animal, but feeling none of the things which were happening to her, on account of her hope and firm hold upon what had been entrusted to her, and her communion with Christ, she also was sacrificed. And the heathen themselves confessed that never among them had a woman endured so many and such terrible tortures."

Like her Lord, she endured all things "for the joy that was set before her … despising the shame," aware of the great cloud of witnesses who were watching her trial. And who can doubt that when God at last allowed her frail body to take its last breath, she was immediately surrounded in heaven by the glad welcoming cries of all those who had so recently gone before her, and joined them in praising the Savior, her dear Master, whom she now saw face to face.

DEVOTIONAL THOUGHT

The story of Blandina reminds us that the Lord gives power and grace to all who need it, and that power shows up brightest in the darkest trials. Whatever the Lord may call you to endure, he will give you the strength to face it if you seek his help. Only be faithful to hold on to Jesus, no matter how anyone threatens you or persecutes you.

We see several examples of this in God's Word. Both David and Gideon were victorious warriors. But David was not an experienced soldier. Where did his strength come from? David tells us himself in the challenging words he spoke to Goliath: "You come against me with sword and spear and javelin, but I come against you in the name of the LORD Almighty" (1 Samuel 17:45 NIV)

Gideon was from the smallest tribe in Israel, yet he was chosen to lead God's army against the Midianites. Was this a large army? No. It was only 300 men.

The Bible tells us that God chooses to use weak people in order to shame the strong (1 Corinthians 1:27) and in Zechariah 4:6 (NIV) it says, "Not by might, nor by power but by my Spirit says the LORD Almighty."

These are good things for us to remember as we live and work in a world that is hostile to Jesus Christ and God's Word. We may be weak, but God is strong and he has already won this great battle against sin and the devil.

FACT FILE

Gaul was a region of Western Europe during the Iron Age and Roman era, encompassing present day France, Luxembourg and Belgium, most of Switzerland, Northern Italy, as well as the parts of the Netherlands and Germany on the west bank of the Rhine.

Lyon, or Lyons as it is now called, is a city in east-central France in the Rhône-Alpes region, situated between Paris and Marseille. The residents of the city are called Lyonnais.

In Lyons there are two large hills, one to the west and one to the north. To the west is a hill called Fourvière. It is referred to as "the hill that prays." This is the location of several convents and other church buildings. To the north is the hill called Croix-Rousse, also known as "the hill that works." This area was traditionally the area where there were many small silk workshops, an industry for which the city was once renowned.

THE DANGER OF DELIVERANCE:

Constantine (AD 274–337)

The general got up early as usual, but something about him had radically changed. He began giving orders left and right, so that his men could prepare for battle. That was not so strange, except that this time, Constantine was asking that a symbol be painted on all the shields of all his men. It was a symbol that a lot of the soldiers would have known, but one that they mostly kept secret: the Chi Rho, or the first two letters of the name of "Christ."

The army was usually known as sun worshipers (not in the sense that they laid around on the beach all day, but that they worshiped the god of the sun). But, more and more, Christians were rising up in all different parts of the society—even in the armies that had been persecutors of the Christians for the last several decades.

What was happening today was going to affect the course of history for the next thousand years. The general Constantine was not just a general, but a contender to be the Roman Emperor in the West. He claimed he had a right to rule the empire all by himself, but at this time, there were several people

ruling parts of the empire, and they all wanted more of the pie! The main person standing in Constantine's way was Maxentius, who had taken over the city of Rome, and was in the battlefield before Constantine with twice as many troops, at a place called Milvian Bridge. Before going out, Maxentius had gone to a Pagan prophetess to find out how the battle would turn out, and had been told, vaguely enough, that today "the enemy of Rome" would die. Happy with this, he marched out confident of victory.

Constantine told others that he had a vision that night. He saw in the sky the letters we mentioned before, and he heard a voice say, "In this sign, conquer." He also said that Jesus told him to put this symbol on the shields and fight for his cause. To him, that meant that he was to make his army Christians, and fight in the name of the Lord Jesus Christ, who would give them the victory! Now, you can probably already see that there is a little bit of a problem. Constantine thought Christianity was just like the pagan religions. He thought of it as something you just told everyone to suddenly be. Often people who were threatened changed their religion in order to save their lives. Constantine didn't have a problem with this. In fact this mindset in Constantine stayed with him for a long time.

However, once the shields were painted and the soldiers baptized, the battle was a great success, even though the men were heavily outnumbered. Constantine thought this confirmed that he really should favor the Christian religion and be a Christian himself.

After the famous victory at Milvian Bridge in AD 312, the Roman senate declared that he was a great deliverer of the people, and officially established him as the emperor of the Roman Empire in the West. Along with his fellow emperor in the East, Licinius, Constantine signed the Edict of Milan in AD 313. This was a statement saying that Christians must be tolerated, and cannot be persecuted. For the first time from the birth of the church in the days of the

Apostles, Christianity was officially proclaimed as a protected religion in the Roman Empire. For the next 1,000 years after Constantine, there would still be brief periods of persecution under other rulers, but the amount of persecution and the type of persecution were very different. The church in the West (where the Roman Empire was) experienced much more peace than in its earliest years.

Whatever may have happened that night when Constantine said he saw the Chi Rho, God ultimately was at work to stop the persecutions, which brought a whole new set of challenges for the church to deal with. His people needed to learn not only how to face

times of hardship, but also how to live in prosperity and peace. As well, the church needed to learn how to deal with well-meaning people who wanted to decide its doctrines and policies.

So, where did Constantine come from, and what did he do after he was made emperor? Constantine was born in the Roman province of Moesia, and named Flavius Valerius Constantinus. Just to be confusing, his father was Flavius Constantius, an officer in the Roman army, and a bodyguard to the emperor. His mother was a Greek named Helena, who may have been a true believer in Christ, and helped to influence her famous son in his decision to become a Christian himself.

As Constantine grew into adulthood, his dad became a governor, and then a kind of "junior emperor" under Diocletian. Constantine became a soldier while still very young, and was soon taking part in various campaigns against Diocletian's enemies. Some of these were enemies of the Roman Empire, such as the Persians and the barbarians, but sadly, Diocletian was also a violent hater of Christianity, and in AD 303 he started up the "Great Persecution" against Christians that was to become notorious as the worst one in Roman history, killing thousands and thousands of believers.

In later years, Constantine always said he took no hand in the persecution, and while this may be true, it is also evident that he did nothing of any significance to stop it, or to help the Christians enduring it. After Constantine became emperor and proclaimed his attachment to Christianity, his political enemies were very fond of bringing up how he had sat around twiddling his thumbs while Christ's followers perished.

But God was still on his throne during the persecution, and within a few years he knocked the emperor Diocletian off of his! Diocletian became so ill, he couldn't rule anymore, and he divided up the empire into several sections ruled by different leaders. These leaders all started fighting each other for the next seven years, leading to the battle we mentioned earlier in AD 312. However, once Constantine won power in the West another problem sprang up. His last remaining rival, Licinius, broke the agreement to tolerate Christians and began to persecute believers in the east. So, Constantine went to war against him. It became a battle of "Christians" against "Pagans," as Licinius gathered around him Goth (or barbarian) mercenaries. At the end of this war, Constantine, though outnumbered on occasion, had won three major battles, and ended up as the sole emperor of the Roman Empire in AD 324.

Christians saw this as a great victory, since this was the most tolerant person they ever had to serve under. He was a hero in most Christians' eyes, and even long after his death. Indeed, he seems to have meant well for Christians, but it isn't clear whether he really understood some of the major doctrines of the faith. We have to remember, though, that for an emperor even to say they were a Christian was amazing. It would be like a leader in Communist China claiming to be a disciple of Jesus, when this country (among many others) has been atheistic and has persecuted thousands of Christians to this day. Maybe God will do such a thing again in some of the persecuted countries like China!

So Constantine became the first "Christian" emperor. He made it the official religion of the empire, and in writing to Christians he always gave God the credit for bringing him to a position of power. He promoted believers in the government, and built churches, and took a close interest in keeping the church doctrine free of heresy. When controversy over the teachings of Arius became too violent, Constantine called together the Council of Nicaea, which was a gathering of 318 church leaders from all over the Empire.

Unfortunately, Constantine also did a number of things that make one wonder at what point in his life he may truly have been converted. For instance, as emperor he kept a lot of pagan practices, but made a "Christian" version of them. This was part of what led to the church having a lot of traditions that can't be supported by the Bible. And since he favored believers, the churches weren't very eager to stand against Constantine's ideas. Furthermore, he delayed being baptized until he knew he was dying, and then, he chose one of the "Arian"[1] bishops to do it. Earlier, Constantine had supported Athanasius and those bishops who believed in the full deity of Christ. But later the emperor allowed himself to be persuaded by the smooth speeches of Arius and his friends, and, was even responsible for exiling the godly Athanasius.

All in all, the life of Constantine was a very important one for the history of the church, but also a rather confusing one from a personal point of view. Was he a true believer, or did he just find the religion of Christ politically useful? With the writings that have survived down through the centuries, it is impossible for anyone to say for sure. We must be content to leave the state of his soul with the All-Knowing God. What we can take positively from Constantine's history is the determination to live our own lives in such a way that hundreds of years from now, if anybody is reading about us and trying to figure out our motivations, they will not spend even a moment asking, "Was he or wasn't he a Christian?" or "Did she or did she not love Christ?" Even if those

---

[1] Arian – a person who follows the theological teaching of Arius who believed that Jesus did not always exist with the Father, but was created out of nothing..

people reading about us are God's enemies, we want them to say, "Well, there's no doubt about it! This person was fanatical about serving Christ and didn't care about anything else."

If only, instead of just "In this sign Conquer," Constantine had more fully realized that "in this Person" we must "LIVE"!

DEVOTIONAL THOUGHT

There are examples in the Bible of kings who started off well, but ended badly. King Solomon began his reign by asking God to give him wisdom instead of riches, but later in his life he left the worship of the one true God to follow the faith of his idolatrous wives. King Saul was the first monarch of Israel and appeared to be a good choice. However, he also wandered away from the one true God. The young King Joash was rescued from certain death by Jehosheba and was brought up to worship God by the Priest Jehoida. However, when Jehoida died, Joash turned away from God.

It is sad to read of great men making these terrible choices. Other kings however, like David, made wrong choices and repented of them. We need to be careful about the choices we make. If you have been brought up to follow God, like Joash, you need to trust and follow the Lord Jesus Christ for yourself. You can't rely on someone else's faith to get you to heaven, or on what you have been taught in the past. You need to trust in the Lord and have a personal relationship with him. You need to repent of your sin, like David did and "bear fruits in keeping with repentance" (Luke 3:8 ESV).

FACT FILE

Constantine the Great was also known as Constantine I or Saint Constantine. He was Roman Emperor from AD 306 to AD 337 and defeated the emperors Maxentius and Licinius during civil wars. Constantine built a new imperial residence at Byzantium, naming it New Rome. However, in Constantine's honor, people called it Constantinople, which would later be the capital of the Eastern Roman Empire for over one thousand years. The modern name for this city is Istanbul.

THE LIFE AND DEATH OF MR. BADMAN:

Arius (AD 256–336)

The emperor Constantine acted in ways that have made people wonder, to this day, whether he was a true Christian. But there is no doubt about Arius—he was a wolf in sheep's clothing! Diocletian killed and tortured Christians and took away their property. Arius was even more dangerous, since he worked inside the church, claiming to be a Christian himself. With his lies about Christ, he deceived many men. They were led to believe false things about the

Savior, and because of this unbelief they would not have been redeemed.

Arius taught that the Lord Jesus was not really God, and that while God the Father had always existed, Christ was just a creature "made from nothing." Arius came up with his teachings not by reading the Bible, of course, but by taking bits and pieces out of the writings of some Christian scholars, who had become confused about the nature of God. The Council of Nicaea, which came about because of the turmoil created by Arius and his followers, helped the church leaders by setting down, very plainly, what the true church believed and taught about the

nature of God—Father, Son, and Holy Spirit. So in this way, though he certainly did not intend to do so, Arius was a means of helping the church become stronger and more Christ-honoring.

It's tempting to think that a man who told such hateful lies would look evil, and slither around with a sneaky walk and a serpent-like hiss in his voice. But that's not how the devil is, and it isn't how Arius was either. He was a brilliant and witty man, which made people like him. Tall and handsome, he was attractive to ladies as well, who loved his "beautiful manners" and gentlemanly ways. Arius also was good at writing and singing. He had a way of putting songs to a catchy beat that made them easy to remember. In fact, his songs became a way to try to get his bad teaching into people's minds. For example, he would sing about how "there was a time when he was not," and the he was Jesus. Arius was trying to subtly teach people that Jesus had not always existed with the Father, which is the opposite of what the Bible teaches (John 1:1-5). The church Arius grew up in was the same one as Athanasius. He was a deacon while Athanasius was an elder—until Athanasius and others expressed concern about his teaching, that is. But Arius' songs were still charming to people. Some probably didn't understand how bad these songs were, since they sounded so good. But his songs were so dangerous and tempting to people that, for a time, Athanasius banned all singing in the church!

But however fascinating and distinguished Arius was, all the brilliant words he could come up with could not change the fact that, if Christ was only a creature, he could not have paid for our sins, and so everybody in the world was still condemned to eternal punishment by God's Holy Law. That was the main point that Athanasius made against Arius. But Arius continued to charm a lot of people into forgetting this! Even after the Council of Nicaea, where his teachings were formally condemned, Arius

did not give up and admit he was wrong. He toned down his teachings a bit, so they wouldn't be quite as shocking, but he didn't abandon them, not for a minute—he just got sneakier. Though he acted like he would submit to the church's decision, he bided his time, gathering enough supporters to make the emperor Constantine reconsider the Council's decision in favor of the full deity of Christ. Bit by bit, over the course of about ten years, Arius and his friends wormed their way back into positions of power; bit by bit, Constantine allowed himself to be persuaded into looking on the Arians with

favor. Finally, in 336, the emperor allowed Arius to return from banishment, and ordered Athanasius to welcome Arius back into good standing in the church. The emperor's wife played a big part in this, since she supported Arius. There was a statement given that made it look like Arius had taken back his words, but this cunning and deceitful man was still the same. Of course, Athanasius the shepherd of the church in Alexandria wasn't about to let a wolf into the flock! He saw through this apparent change of heart, and refused to accept Arius back, since there was no real change in his beliefs. In response, the emperor exiled Athanasius.

Can you picture the triumph of Arius and his followers? The emperor had once again flip-flopped onto the wrong side, and Arius was looking forward to many years of teaching his false doctrine with the emperor's approval. Pride swelled up in his heart at the thought of a sweet victory, with Athanasius gone, and him and his songs enchanting the people once again!

But though the emperor supported Arius' return, the God of heaven did not. For many years he had permitted Arius to tell his lies unharmed, and had even sent his servants Alexander and Athanasius to warn Arius of his errors, and the judgment for them. But proud Arius had not paid any attention, and now God's patience had come to an end and his judgment was ripe.

After he got the official word from the emperor that he could return to the church, Arius left Constantine's palace, surrounded by people who had believed his teaching and thought of him as a hero. Arius was like a rock star, and his fans were ready to escort him back to the church, parading through the city, making sure that all the people around took note of what was happening. Then suddenly, as Arius was approaching a place called Constantine's Forum, he was seized by a violent pain and illness. You know how you feel when you have eaten something bad, or had the flu, and your stomach hurts, and you feel like being sick, and all you want to do is get to the nearest bathroom? That seems to be what happened to Arius. His big parade had to be stopped, and his friends took him to a private place off the street somewhere. But there was no relief for him, for this was no ordinary sickness. His insides were all wrong, and so diseased that his body was trying to expel them! Soon he grew faint, and he began bleeding horribly, and he died there in the middle of his city, on the way to the church. Arius tried to rob Christ of his deity, and was dramatically judged before the horrified eyes of his followers. For years, it is said, people would point to the very place where Arius had been struck down, and talk about his sudden destruction at the very moment when it seemed he had triumphed in teaching these errors.

However gross and unpleasant it is to hear, these kinds of events are displays of the terrible wrath of God against those who afflict the church—from within or from without. His death reminds us of some of the wicked men in the Bible who died suddenly and in great pain due to their unrepentant rebellion against God (See Jehoram in 2 Chronicles 21:12-20, and Herod in Acts 12:1-4, 20-25). These horrible earthly judgments are a warning of the greater eternal judgment for those who do not give glory to the Son of God. The Father is righteously jealous that his Son is glorified on equal terms with him (John 5:19-23). The church saw how seriously God hates lies about his Son when Arius was killed in the street that day.

DEVOTIONAL THOUGHT

The Bible warns us about evil and those who teach it. The Apostle Peter says:

> "But there were also false prophets among the people, just as there will be false teachers among you. They will secretly introduce destructive heresies, even denying the sovereign Lord who bought them—bringing swift destruction on themselves" (2 Peter 2:1 NIV).

So what do we do to protect ourselves from false teaching? We daily, thoughtfully, study the Scripture. The Bereans were a good example of this. When Paul came to teach them, they made sure that what he said matched the Word of God. They did this by comparing all that he said with the scriptures. You can read about this in Acts chapter 17.

Perhaps you are concerned about how to tell the difference between a godly person and an ungodly person. The Bible tells us that whoever knows God listens to the teaching of the apostles and prophets found in God's Word, but those who don't know him deny, reject, or twist the Bible's message:

> "This is how we recognize the Spirit of truth and the spirit of falsehood" (1 John 4:6 NIV).

FACT FILE

Nicaea was the capital city of the Byzantine Empire between 1204 and 1261. The ancient city is located within modern Turkey at the eastern end of Lake Ascanius. In AD 325, during the reign of Constantine, the First Council of Nicaea was held and the Nicene Creed drawn up. The early church's confession of the doctrine of the Trinity was finalized at the Council of Constantinople in AD 381 which included the Holy Ghost as equal to the Father and the Son.

ONE NIGHT
ON THE NILE:

Athanasius (c. AD 293–373)

A thanasius was on the run! The emperor had become convinced that he was causing too much trouble. This was not the only time they had attempted to arrest him. On another occasion, when his church members saw that the soldiers were coming to get him, they surrounded him and started singing in a big group in the street, like Christmas carolers! That time, Athanasius was able to slip out through his friends and into the crowd, escaping the soldiers in the midst of a bustling street scene. But now it was different. He was on the run at night, and with just a couple of friends with him. They were making their way down the famous Nile River, and Athanasius knew that these Roman soldiers were stronger and faster, and that their boat would soon catch up with them. As they turned around a bend in the river, they knew their time was short and the distance between them and their hunters was closing. Suddenly, Athanasius had an idea! He told the men rowing the boat to turn around and head back for Alexandria.

They couldn't believe their ears! Had he gone mad? Did he want to turn himself in? I can imagine there were some arguments, but Athanasius would not hear of it. Smiling, he told his companions, "He who is for us is greater than he who is against us."

Soon they could hear the sounds of the imperial boats approaching on the other side of the wide river. The oarsman with Athanasius were terrified, knowing any minute the soldiers would see them and seize their little boat and probably arrest them all. Once the soldiers had seen them, and the imperial boat was

slowing down a little, one of the men at the head of the boat leaned toward them, shouting and gesturing. What was he saying? "Have you seen Athanasius?" the soldier demanded harshly. "Is he far off?" The men at the oars trembled, and looked at each other silently, wondering who should speak. Then, to their amazement and horror, they heard Athanasius calling back calmly to the soldier: "He is quite close ... press on!" We can't help but wonder if that commander bothered to shout across a hasty "thank you," as his men once more began rowing forward at full speed, determined to catch up with the boat that had gone out of sight around the bend!

That was just one adventurous night among many in the life of Athanasius. As well as escaping from the Imperial Guard–over the course of his life, he was exiled five times! By this point in church history, the Roman Empire had undergone a great change, and the emperor had declared Christianity a legal religion. So, why was Athanasius being chased out of town? That's a good question. The main answer is that though Christians weren't persecuted as before, the empire was not suddenly Christian, and the emperors often didn't have a very good idea of what Christianity was either. So even in an empire where Christianity had become accepted, there was still trouble for those who held fast to what Scripture said about Jesus. Athanasius was one of those people. He loved the truth—in fact, he spent most of his life fighting for the truth that Jesus truly is God, equal to the Father and worthy of worship and praise.

Athanasius, was raised in Alexandria. He came to the attention of church leaders while still very young.

The story is told that Alexander, Bishop of Alexandria, saw Athanasius playing "church" with some other boys, and pretending to baptize them, and so the bishop helped get Athanasius and his friends into training to become true church leaders. When Athanasius grew older, he became Alexander's secretary, and eventually he would become Bishop of Alexandria himself. But when Athanasius was still only a deacon, a man named Arius began to teach that the Lord Jesus was not truly God, eternal and unchangeable, but that he had come into existence at a certain time, and was therefore inferior to God the Father.

Bishop Alexander and many others opposed his teachings, denouncing him as a heretic, but there were also many men, some of them bishops, who believed that Arius was right.

Athanasius stood with Alexander in defense of the deity of the Lord Jesus, and wrote a famous book, which is still read today, called *The Incarnation of the Word of God*. Many people were convinced by it, but the disagreement that Arius stirred up by his teachings was huge. Not only church leaders, but emperors became involved through the years, some taking one side, and some another. In AD 325 the emperor Constantine called a council of all the most important church leaders. They were to meet at a place called Nicaea (a town in Turkey), and talk about the different doctrines being taught until enough of them came to an agreement on the truth. This eventually happened and the church leaders sent out a document to the churches saying, "This is what true Christians believe." It took a while, and there were many bitter arguments, but the First Council of Nicaea, as it was called, finally came up with a statement for the churches, known as the Nicene Creed. It is a very famous and important Christian statement, and the first part of it goes like this:

> I believe in one God, the Father Almighty, Maker of heaven and earth, and of all things visible and invisible.

> And in one Lord Jesus Christ, the only-begotten Son of God, begotten of the Father before all worlds; God of God, Light of Light, very God of very God; begotten, not made, being of one substance with the Father, by whom all things were made.

> Who, for us men and for our salvation, came down from heaven, and was incarnate by the Holy Spirit of the virgin Mary, and was made man; and

74

was crucified also for us under Pontius Pilate; He suffered and was buried; and the third day He rose again, according to the Scriptures; and ascended into heaven, and sits on the right hand of the Father; and He shall come again, with glory, to judge the quick and the dead; whose kingdom shall have no end.

As you might expect, Arius and his followers were not very happy with this outcome! They refused to submit to the judgment of the council, and continued to teach their lies about the Lord Jesus. They were especially angry with Athanasius, who while still a very young man had written the accusation against Arius that had made Alexander depose him. Then, at the Council, his arguments had been some of the most persuasive and powerful, so that out of 300 bishops, only two refused to sign the agreement and adopt the new creed.

Some of the bishops who had signed the Nicene Creed were still a little afraid of speaking out too strongly against the "Arians," as they were called, but Athanasius did not hesitate to call a spade a spade. What Arius taught was a lie, and blasphemy against the Lord Jesus Christ, and so Arius was a heretic, and that was that! Naturally, this did not make Athanasius many friends among the Arians.

Ten years after the Council at Nicaea, they called another meeting and accused Athanasius of mistreating Arians and some of their allies, members of another sect called Melitians. They said that he was also threatening the prosperity of the empire, and got the emperor Constantine to banish him. After that, Athanasius was recalled to favor and then banished again several times, depending on the whim of the emperor reigning at the time. Through it all, Athanasius continued to write his books in defense of the faith. Once when he was exiled he found refuge with some monks who lived in the desert, and he was so impressed by one of them, named Anthony, that he wrote a biography of the man, which became a very famous work, and greatly influenced another great Christian leader and theologian, Augustine.

But Athanasius was not content to hide and write; he wanted to be serving God's people, and teaching them the truths of the gospel. He wanted nothing more than for the church to be unified in belief, and to live peacefully and lovingly with one another as Christians should, but he was not willing to sacrifice the truth to make the Arians happy. Time after time he would return to Alexandria when his persecutors died, or when his friends managed to talk an emperor into recalling him, and time after time his enemies would rise against him and he'd have to leave once more.

At the very end of his life, Athanasius was at last granted several years of peace, in which he did his best, by his writings and preaching, to heal all the damage done to the church by all the years of fighting and controversy. However, he had been accused and exiled so many times in his life, that when he died, the words that were carved on his tombstone were "Athanasius contra mundum," meaning "Athanasius against the world." This was a testimony to the fact that even if everyone else in the world was against him, Athanasius was a man who stood faithfully for what he believed to be true.

DEVOTIONAL THOUGHT

> I believe in one God, the Father Almighty, Maker
> of heaven and earth, and of all things visible and
> invisible.

Make a list of things that come to mind when you think of the words, "visible and invisible." This is a good phrase to use when describing what God has made. It covers everything, doesn't it?

When this creed was being written there were a lot of things that hadn't been discovered. They weren't yet visible to the human eye. There were galaxies and planets that nobody had seen. And it's the same today. Scientists are always discovering new stars. When Athanasius was alive there were parts of the body, cells and DNA, that no one knew existed. Even today scientists keep making new biological discoveries. If we could read the science text books of the future we'd be greatly surprised at all the new and wonderful things written there about the human body. Science is wonderful because God is wonderful.

God has made all of creation from the giant black holes in outer space to the small motors ingeniously built into every single cell; from powerful whales and elephants to tiny, fragile humming birds and butterflies. God has made planets that dwarf our own little planet in size – but he has also made everything that you need to look at through a microscope.

The Nicene Creed expresses this very well. But so does the Bible. That's how we can determine if something written and devised by mankind follows the will of God – we check the Scriptures. Here's a verse from the Bible that backs up the fact that God has made everything visible and invisible.

> "For in him all things were created: things in heaven and on earth, visible and invisible, whether thrones or powers or rulers or authorities; all things have been created through him and for him" (Colossians 1:16 NIV).

We can trust God's Word because we can trust God. His Word is true because he is true and unlike you and me, human beings who are sinful and weak, God is unchanging. So we can rely on what he says because we can rely on him – the one who is the same yesterday, today and forever.

FACT FILE

The Nile is a major river in northeastern Africa. It is 6,650 km (4,130 miles) long. It runs through the countries of Sudan, South Sudan, Burundi, Rwanda, Democratic Republic of the Congo, Tanzania, Kenya, Ethiopia, Uganda and Egypt.

The Nile has two major tributaries, the White Nile and Blue Nile. The White Nile is longer and rises in the Great Lakes region of central Africa. The Blue Nile is the source of most of the water and fertile soil. It begins at Lake Tana in Ethiopia and flows into Sudan from the southeast. The two rivers meet near the Sudanese capital of Khartoum.

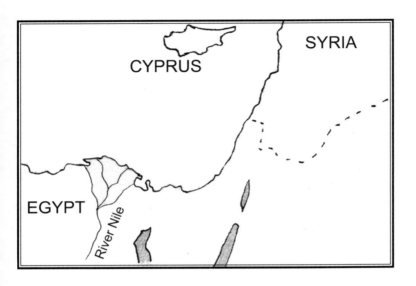

ALL MEANS ALL:
Anthony (AD 251–356)

One of the most popular books of the Middle Ages was one called *The Life of Anthony*. God used this book in the conversion of Augustine. It was written by Athanasius during one of those times when he had made the emperor mad and been forced to leave Alexandria, and this time he had decided to go to a desert in Egypt to hide out for a while. While he was there he met Anthony, who was already well-known for his wisdom and his simple lifestyle. He had given up the pursuit of riches and sought to take seriously (maybe too seriously!) the call to be separate from the world. Athanasius was so impressed with Anthony's radical discipleship that he wrote a biography of him, and told churches in the east, including the church in Rome, about Anthony's godliness and example, urging them to follow his pattern. The emperor Constantine had even written a letter to him, asking for his blessing! (Anthony tried to ignore it, but his friends wouldn't let him, and eventually he broke down and agreed to write back to the emperor.)

So, how did a man who spent more than fifty years running away from people and trying to live without distractions, come to the notice of the emperor?

This is what Athanasius says happened: When Anthony was a boy in Egypt, his parents were very wealthy, but when he was still a teenager they died and he was left to care for his young sister. His parents were both Christians, and Anthony had grown up attending church and knowing the gospel. A few months after his parents died, as he was heading to church, he was thinking about all that he had inherited from them, and about how the Apostles had left everything to follow Christ (Matthew 19:24-29). He considered how later disciples had even sold everything they had to share with their brethren (Acts 4:32-37). With these things on his mind, he arrived at the church, and walked in just as someone was reading from the Bible the Lord's words to the rich young ruler:

> Jesus said to him, "If you want to be perfect, go, sell what you have and give to the poor, and you will have treasure in heaven; and come, follow Me" (Matthew 19:21 NKJV).

Anthony felt that these words were being spoken directly to him. He turned around and immediately set about selling everything he had, to give to the poor. At first he kept back enough to take care of his sister, but then the next day he went back to church and heard them reading "do not be anxious about tomorrow," so he promptly went out and gave away that too, placing his sister with a group of Christian women to look after her. Anthony was convicted that when Jesus says to give him "all," he really means all!

Then, Anthony went to live a very simple life with a local hermit. (Of course, he didn't have much choice but to live simply, since he didn't own anything anymore!) Now that he had gotten rid of all his "worldliness," young Anthony thought he would certainly be holy and "pleasing to God."

Unfortunately, Anthony soon found out that though he could leave behind his worldly possessions, he could not leave behind his soul, and so his worldly, sinful thoughts followed him out to the desert. He was bored, he didn't have much to do, but he didn't even want to do those things, and he kept thinking of all the girls he'd left behind! This was not working at all! He was supposed to be thinking of nothing but God, but still these temptations arose. He prayed and prayed, and eventually decided that the best thing to do was to find a nice tomb to live in; there, surely, he would be motivated by his surroundings to think of nothing but God. So, he found a burial cave to stay in. The local villagers brought him food, impressed that such a spiritual man had chosen to live near them.

The tomb, however, did not work out well either. Anthony still struggled with his sinful thoughts, sometimes violently. One time, when the villagers came out to him, they found him unconscious— everyone thought the devil himself must have beaten Anthony up because he was so enraged by Anthony's holy life! The villagers brought him to a church to recover his health, but as soon as he could, Anthony left again, this time going far out into the desert, where he shut himself up in an old abandoned Roman Fort. There, it seemed to him that he was constantly threatened by wild beasts and scorpions trying to

kill him, but he believed these were but phantoms sent by the devil, and he laughed at them until they went away. But while the wild beasts might leave him alone, people would not: they started coming all the way out to the desert to get his advice, and even though he refused to let them in, they would press up against the small hole where his food was handed into him, and listen to what he had to say. They were amazed at his insights, sure that any man locked up alone like that for so long would go insane.

But Anthony did not lose his reason. Instead, one day he decided to come out and pay a visit to some churches, sharing what he had learned, shut up alone with God. (The villagers helped him break down the door he had sealed up.) All the people could not believe how healthy and peaceful he seemed, and how everything he said seemed filled with wisdom. He didn't stay out for long, but after doing what he could to strengthen the church, he returned to his Fort.

In AD 311, however, Anthony had another idea. Living alone on bread and water and worshiping God full time was not enough: the ultimate way to glorify him would be to die for him. The church was in a season of persecution, and Anthony didn't want to be hiding in the desert like a coward while his brothers and sisters suffered. He went to help and support the church in Alexandria during their time of suffering. Since he had already given himself wholly to the Lord, he was more than willing to die for him. He tried his best to stir up the officials there into martyring him, but though the governor complained that Anthony was speaking about Christianity openly, and tried to get him to leave the city, no one was willing to kill him over it. He'd succeeded in helping the church, but failed in seeking martyrdom, so Anthony went back to his Fort in the desert.

Now, he was more popular than ever. People continued to travel out to speak to him. So, Anthony tried moving even further into the desert. But still, people followed him to get his insights into the Christian life.

At last, he settled in a place with water and some palm trees. By this time he seems to have given up on the idea of being completely alone, and actually allowed some disciples to come and stay and learn from him. Together they prayed and worked in their gardens, and wove rush mats when they were bored (which I imagine was quite frequently). They also gave advice to any hardy souls that managed to make it out to speak to them—though Anthony refused to have anything to do with worldly people who just came out of curiosity and not true spiritual need. He let one of his disciples deal with those!

Eventually, a monastery was built on this spot, which still stands there today. Although Anthony never achieved his ideal of perfect solitude and worship of God every minute of every day, he did succeed in paring down his life to the very basics. And he kept working for the Lord throughout his life. Since he was greatly respected, Athanasius asked him to help battle the false doctrine of the Arians, so he left his retreat again when he was around 100 years old (he lived to be 105). He did a lot to help the church see the importance of believing in the deity of Christ, which was a great way to spend the last years of his life.

When Anthony died, he asked to be buried in a secret grave, but even in death, he could not escape people's determination to find him. His grave was "discovered" a few years later and moved to Alexandria, and then eventually was moved to France, where, as often happened in the Middle Ages, a lot of stories grew up about how his remains had brought about miracles of healing. So, people took trips to visit his tomb. Poor Anthony! They even pestered his grave after he had gone on to glory!

DEVOTIONAL THOUGHT

Much of what we read about Anthony sounds strange. He wants to give everything to the Lord and to prayer - yet wherever he goes he can't seem to avoid temptation. Even when things are going well he can't avoid other people - no matter how far he tries to go. But what a way to end his life:

> He did a lot to help the church see the importance
> of believing in the deity of Christ.

It is important to start well, but also to end well. The Christian life is not just one moment when we say "Yes" to God - it should be a whole lifetime of saying "Yes." Like Anthony, we're never going to be able to avoid temptation, but the Bible tells us that we can flee our evil desires and pursue righteousness. Read 2 Timothy 2:22.

We don't need to leave the world and live alone to be holy. We need to draw near to God. And we also need to have good fellowship with other believers to strengthen us in the Lord.

FACT FILE

The land of Egypt has had quite a few different names. The English name Egypt has its roots in ancient Greek and Latin as well as other languages such as Arabic.

Misr is the modern official name of Egypt. The ancient Egyptian name of the country is Kemet which means "black land," referring to the fertile black soils of the Nile flood plains. Egypt is the fifteenth most populated country in the world. Most of its 82 million people live near the banks of the Nile River, an area of about 40,000 square kilometers (15,000 square miles).

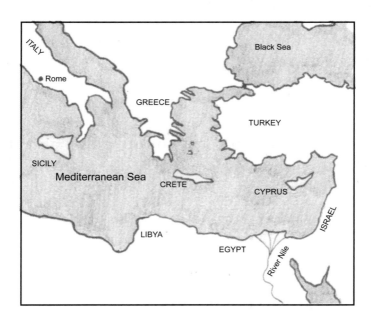

QUIZ: POLYCARP

1. Which disciple of Jesus did Polycarp study under?

2. In what modern day country did Polycarp pastor?

3. What was Polycarp doing when the soldiers arrived?

4. How was Polycarp killed?

5. What is one explanation for how Smyrna got its name?

QUIZ: BLANDINA

1. What modern-day country was Blandina from?

2. Who was the emperor at the time of Blandina's arrest?

3. What was the name of the fifteen-year-old boy Blandina helped in the arena?

4. What animal was used to kill Blandina?

5. What industry was the city of Lyon famous for?

QUIZ: CONSTANTINE

1. What was the name of the symbol painted on the soldiers' shields?

2. At what bridge did the famous battle take place?

3. In what year did Constantine become Emperor of Rome?

4. What was the name of the council that Constantine called together?

5. What is the modern name for Constantinople?

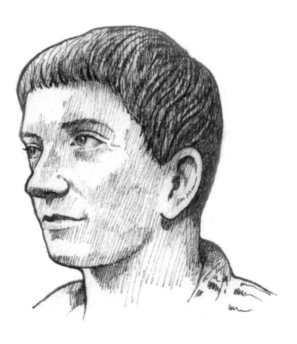

QUIZ: ARIUS

1. What false teaching did Arius teach?

2. Which of Arius' talents did he use for spreading false teaching?

3. What did Athanasius do in the church to combat Arius' false teaching?

4. What horrible thing happened during the parade?

5. What doctrine was finalised at the Council of Constantinople in AD 381?

QUIZ: ATHANASIUS

1. How did Athanasius' friends help him avoid arrest on the street?

2. How did Athanasius first come to the notice of the Bishop of Alexandria?

3. What is the name of the creed that was written in AD 325?

4. Which two groups did Athanasius disagree with?

5. What was written on Athanasius' tomb stone?

QUIZ: ANTHONY

1. Who read a book about Anthony that was written by Athanasius?

2. What did Anthony do after he sold all his possessions?

3. Why did Anthomy go to Alexandria in AD 311?

4. How old was Anthony when he died?

5. What important doctrine did Anthony support?

QUIZ ANSWERS

POLYCARP

1. John

2. Turkey

3. Asleep in bed

4. Burned alive

5. It's the ancient Greek name for the gum/resin myrrh

BLANDINA

1. France

2. Marcus Aurelius

3. Ponticus

4. A bull

5. Silk weaving

CONSTANTINE

1. Chi Rho

2. Milvian Bridge

3. AD 324

4. Council of Nicaea

5. Istanbul

ARIUS

1. He falsely taught that Jesus was not God

2. Song writing

3. He banned singing

4. Arius died a painful death

5. The doctrine of the Trinity

ATHANASIUS

1. They surrounded him and sang

2. He and his friends were playing church

3. The Nicene Creed

4. The Arians and the Melitians

5. "Athanasius against the World"

ANTHONY

1. Augustine

2. Became a hermit

3. To help the church and become a martyr

4. 105

5. The deity of Christ

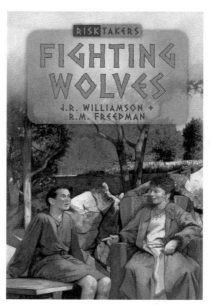

Fighting Wolves by J.R. Williamson
and R.M. Freedman
ISBN: 978-1-78191-154-9

Wolves have had a bit of a Public Relations campaign lately. If fairy tales were being written today the wolf would save the three little pigs and escort Little Red Riding Hood to safety. But it wasn't always like that. People in the days of the early church saw wolves as wild predators. That's why the Apostle Paul described the false teachers who sought to destroy Christians as 'savage wolves'. There was great danger in the early church of those false teachers leading Christians into error by teaching lies. So let's go to the very early years of the church to discover the names of those people who fought for and against God's truth. Characters included: The Apostle James; Basil the Great; Ambrose of Milan; Chrysostom; Simeon Stylites; Monica; Augustine.

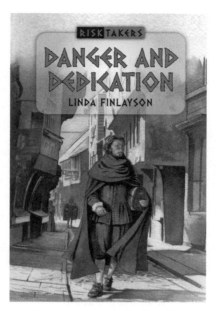

Danger and Dedication
by Linda Finlayson
ISBN: 978-1-84550-587-5

William Tyndale sets about translating the Bible into English. He works in secret and is in constant danger. Adoniram Judson risks his life so that Burmese people can hear the gospel. He is cruelly treated and faces imprisonment. Jonathan Goforth survives an attack by an angry group of rebel Chinese men, but continues to travel and preach to the people of China. Bruce F. Hunt faces imprisonment for refusing to worship the emperor, but God gives him a song to encourage him. Moses meets God at a burning bush and Paul helps build the early church. These men were all willing to take risks. Some even died for what they believed in. With extra devotional features this illustrated book will help young readers to discover the excitement of a Christian life as well as the cost.

Risktakers Series

Adventure and Faith
by Linda Finlayson
ISBN 978-1-84550-491-5

Strength and Devotion
by Linda Finlayson
ISBN 978-1-84550-492-2

Fearless and Faithful
by Linda Finlayson
ISBN 978-1-84550-588-2

Danger and Dedication
by Linda Finlayson
ISBN 978-1-84550-587-5

Fighting Wolves
by J. R. Williamson and R.M. Freedman
ISBN 978-1-78191-154-9

Facing Lions
by J. R. Williamson and R.M. Freedman
ISBN 978-1-78191-153-2

Torchbearers Series

James Chalmers: The Rainmaker's Friend
by Irene Howat
ISBN 978-1-84550-154-9

Jim Elliot: He is no Fool
by Irene Howat
ISBN 978-1-84550-064-1

Nate Saint: Operation Auca
by Nancy Drummond
ISBN 978-1-84550-979-8

Polycarp: The Crown of Fire
by William C Newson
ISBN 978-1-84550-041-2

Titanic: The Ship of Dreams
by Robert Plant
ISBN 978-1-84550-641-4

The Two Margarets: Danger on the Hill
by Catherine Mackenzie
ISBN 978-1-85792-784-9

William Tyndale: The Smuggler's Flame
by Lori Rich
ISBN 978-1-85792-972-0

CHRISTIAN FOCUS PUBLICATIONS

Christian Christian CF4K Mentor
Focus Heritage

Christian Focus Publications publishes books for adults and children under its four main imprints: Christian Focus, CF4K, Mentor and Christian Heritage. Our books reflect our conviction that God's Word is reliable and Jesus is the way to know him, and live for ever with him.

Our children's publication list includes a Sunday School curriculum that covers pre-school to early teens, and puzzle and activity books. We also publish personal and family devotional titles, biographies and inspirational stories that children will love.

If you are looking for quality Bible teaching for children then we have an excellent range of Bible stories and age-specific theological books.

From pre-school board books to teenage apologetics, we have it covered!

**Find us at our web page:
www.christianfocus.com**

CF4•K
*Because you're never
too young to know Jesus*